Mouth
Full of
Seeds

Mouth Full of Seeds

Marcela
Sulak

Black
Lawrence
Press

Black
Lawrence
Press

www.blacklawrence.com

Executive Editor: Diane Goettel
Cover Design: Zoe Norvell
Cover Art: "Black Fields" by Avital Cnaani
Book Design: Amy Freels

Published 2020 by Black Lawrence Press.
Printed in the United States.

Contents

I. Drawn That Way

Drawn That Way

1.
On my birthday my mother writes me: *What is it about you that allows you to pick up, with your little daughter, and leave all your former life behind? Your background, your family, nationality, religion, friends, siblings, parents, your roots. And just start a new life in a new country?*

What freedom of spirit you must have!!

Maybe if Catholic church altars featured statues of Mary with a baby and a book, instead of a crucified, bloody body of a man, I'd have stayed Catholic and become a Catholic Mother in our ancestral homeland, Moravia.

I try to focus on the double exclamation point in *freedom of spirit!!*

2.

I am studying theology at a Jesuit university and discover that the 1905 and 1906 papal commissions on modernism found no legal (as in canon law) reason a woman could not be ordained a priest. But, it was concluded, since God chose to inhabit the body of a man, not a woman, priests should be men, not women.

The most important thing about Jesus' humanity was his genitalia.

Ever after, when I saw a figure of a male hanging from a cross in a church, I would feel waves of nausea. My body would sometimes become wracked in sobs, and I'd have to remove it from the nave. It was embarrassing and puzzling—I certainly wasn't conscious of feeling upset. I liked the candles and incense and ritual and liberation theology.

3.

I loved Mary, the mother. I did not deify the son. This probably would disqualify me from Jewish Motherhood. Luckily I gave birth to a daughter.

4.
I have no idea, Mama, where I got my *freedom of spirit!!*

5.

I meet a man at a wedding. He asks me about my child. Is the father Jewish? It's a question I'd never heard before. I explain that my child's father is Jewish, but I was never married to him. He tells me he is a cohen, that if the father of my child had not been Jewish, well, then maybe…

It sounds sketchy to me, but tell him I am a convert, so it doesn't matter.

He pauses for maybe three beats. He explains the kabbalistic idea that the soul of a convert was always a Jewish soul. It simply got lost and was born into a non-Jewish body. Conversion is *tikkun*. It is making something whole, repairing it, making my body Jewish to house my Jewish soul.

But if the soul was always Jewish, why does my now-Jewish female body become flawed in the presence of your priestly Jewish body?

He has no answer. He is not a scholar.
He would be offended if he knew that at that moment I suddenly had an image of a naked bloody man hanging on a cross.

2 (b).

But there is another way of looking at it—and that is to say that Jesus's body denies the humanity of mine. If Jesus is a human, and my human body could not be priestly, maybe the most important thing about *my* body is the genitalia.

But I know what that Papal Commission on Modernism's conclusion really means, as progressive as I found the mere fact of its existence in 1904 and 1906.

6.

Maybe what I'm getting at here is the sheer physicality of the Mother's Body as a receptacle of life, sure, but of impurity. It shocks me. It always has—simply the physicality of the woman's body. And it continues to shock me after all these years of being alive.

7.

In my perfect world, our thoughts, intentions, emotions, would be visible; our spirits would be visible. We'd see their shape and size and style under our clothes. We'd cover our insecurities with panties or support them with bras. But our ideas would be the physical representations of our selves in the world.

Our bodies, the physical elements, would be accessible only through our minds and our actions. Like the wind —we'd see our bodies only in their movement. When we moved them to fulfill an intention or thought.

8.

"I'm not bad. I'm just drawn that way," says Jessica Rabbit in *Who Framed Roger Rabbit.*

I am drawn that way, too.

9.
When people ask me how I like Israel, if I plan to stay, I say that I am over the angry phase. Over all that bursting into tears when strangers yell at me for no reason in the street. Over asking the neighbors for the tenth time, but this time with a hammer in my hand, to turn down the stereo. (Finally, they do. The silence is astonishing.)

10.
Because in America I was the only tenure-track woman in my university English department who had given birth pre-tenure. Because in Israel I am the only pre-tenure woman in my department who has only one child.

11.

The woman ahead of me at the grocery store in Tel Aviv, furious about an item she'd been over-charged for, shoves her large purse onto the conveyor belt, refusing to bag her groceries. She and the checker exchange loud words, and then the checker checks me out around her. When the checker realizes I don't have a discount card, she freezes. Then she asks the furious woman if she'll lend me her discount card, since, really, I should be saving at least 50 shekels on the bill. "Oh, but of course," the angry woman says, and tells the checker her ID card number. Together they chide me for not getting a card, their argument forgotten.

12.

Today I meet my student to discuss the book she is writing about gender-based violence. *The female body as receptacle for the pain and flaws and sins of the world*, she muses.

Suddenly she explains that the gang rape actually occurred when she was a child. The story she'd shown me about a still-born baby birthed in a toilet stall in school is not, technically, a work of fiction.

She is the second woman I know and love who was gang raped as a child. Both incidents resulted in pregnancy. The other woman's family had had the wherewithal to fly to a country in which abortion was legal. Both women have multiple graduate degrees and supportive families, spiritual, material and intellectual resources. They were raped while in "safe" places.

My student tells me that rape was only conceived of as a crime against a woman about 150 years ago. Previously, rape had been considered a property crime against the woman's father or husband, or to whomever she belonged.

That night I get out of bed and go to my daughter's room. I have been helping craft the "story line" for a documentary about sex trafficking. We have never had a way to secure the balconies in any of the three apartments we've lived in since we moved to Israel. There are no locks on the bedroom doors.

We don't belong to anyone.

13.

The community garden has been closed all week, due to the jackals. Sometimes it is closed because the IDF needs it for something that will, presumably, protect us.

The garden lies past the convergence of the dreamy green Yarkon and the brown Ayalon rivers. It's a 15 minute bike ride along the river from our apartment—past the petting zoo and bird safari, through the little eucalyptus forest that is a national park, just past where the three ancient mills used to be. We pay 180 NIS a month for 40 square meters, which is far too large for us, but my daughter kept shouting, *get the big one! get the big one!* when I was on the phone with the garden people.

Our plot is the most overrun in the entire garden, and I think the other gardeners love us for making them feel so good about themselves in comparison. One has given us sweet-potato clippings, another sunflowers and melon seedlings, another grapes, passion fruit.

I weed for three hours till my hands and shoulders are weak as clouds. It is satisfying. My daughter, for whom this is supposed to be an enriching and wondrous experience, stands next to me and repeats every 90 seconds, *I'm bored when can we go home?*

14.
Pumpkins, zucchini
yellow squash, okra, zinnias
watermelon, sage

cantaloupe, eggplant
heirloom tomatoes, cherry
tomatoes, green beans

basil, hyssop, mint
oregano, cilantro
roses, lemon grass

artichoke, onions
sunflowers, asparagus
yams. Not potatoes.

Now is not the time to plant potatoes.

15.

It finally happens: The Iraqi window repairman's mother can't understand my Hebrew, so I put my six-year-old on so she can translate that it's broken glass and it needs to be replaced. I am ashamed. And yet, it's wonderful to see her pacing up and down with the phone, explaining in detail. Sticking to the facts. Which is more than we can say for the repairman's mother, who is apparently also named Marcela.

My daughter broke the glass. She explains it to the repairman, and that is how I learn she broke the window with her head. She'd told me it was her shoulder. The repairman says that his cousin *died* that way and that we are very, very, very, very lucky.

16.

After the fourth visit to the Ministry of Education to petition that my daughter be returned to the same kindergarten, the only bilingual public one in Tel Aviv, that she was in last year, and *why did they take her out for no reason, and I don't speak Hebrew and I'm a new immigrant and a single mother and I need this school and if they don't put her back I sweartogod I will home-school her, which is actually illegal to do in Israel but I don't care*, and receiving a discouraging non-committal response, I tell the other parents at kindergarten, *I've tried everything I can think of.*

Have you tried crying? every single one of them asks me.

17.

Every time you cry in a government office in Israel you are given a glass of cold water in a disposable plastic cup.

18.
Mommy, are you a girl or a boy? asks my daughter, watching me assemble furniture for the fourth day that week.

I turn the final screw on her bed, *Most definitely a girl.*

Dear Honeysuckled, Dear Fire Department

Dear honeysuckled, dear poison ivy, dear yaupon with your poisoned berries aiming your leaves at random stars and pretending to be pretty, that was me, that was my foot that broke the poison oak, my shoulder that broke the banana-spider web. I forgot what I forgot there, but what you took was mine.

Dear honeysuckled, have all the mosquitoes died? Dear me, how awful it all was, and how familiar. Dear home, how I hated you. How I thought something was missing all that time. Dear me, it was me. I was the missing.

Dear asp in the mustang grapes, dear acid, dear sugar boiling hard, dear mother crying, dear rattle snakes, dear potatoes underneath the house, dear house on its cement blocks, dear crowbar, dear nails, dear wall we ripped out, dear fire that ate you up, dear shotgun shells exploding in the heat, dear fire department, dear deer you were not shot that season.

Dear bobcat killed on the bridge we couldn't swerve to miss, dear creek, dear dredging, dear alligators, dear history of my haunting, I can love almost anything.

Weights and Measures

Many systems of measurement were to some extent based on the dimensions of the human body according to the proportions described by Marcus Vitruvius Pollio. Thus, units of measure could vary from location to location, from person to person.

Whenever the mulberries stained the patio with maps no one read, my cousin Charles lifted me and my brothers, one by one, to the peep show at the telescope, where Saturn's body gleamed through scarves made of years, dust, ice, space, and jeweled with spry, spinning moons. When the honeysuckle wasn't blooming, the garden stank of dog shit. I didn't want to be a girl, a sharp, flat cosmic key good as long as I remained unmarked and never leaked.

While my cousin was talking about cosmic weight, girth, gravity, moons, and rings of ice, my mother was talking about cosmetic weight, girth, gravy spoons and belt size. (Everything relative's related.) My dad and cousin were raised by my aunt as brothers. My cousin studied astronomy and then worked in the Caterpillar warehouse, parts division, which isn't, after all, so different from outer space.

In 1960, the mètre-étalon was replaced as the official measure of the meter. Now a meter is the length of the path traveled by light in a vacuum in 1/299 792 458ths of a second. The expression, to be raised: my cousin always lifting. I've been unjust to my mother. Under the sign of cancer, her breasts are cut away. Now she's the girl she never was, the girl I no longer am.

My cousin died on Thanksgiving Day lifting a fork to his mouth then dropping the fork back. His brother died discussing where to hang a picture in Houston, falling and skewing the frame. I have never been able to maintain placement in time or space. But I've been dreaming the same dream for eight years—that I have a daughter. Before that, I dreamt I was pregnant. My daughter tells me *stop it.*

Cell

Yes, I was one of
a hundred other women
bathing in the film,

I mean the sacred
ritual bath, across the lap
top of the rabbi.

I sent a headshot.
The detective confirmed I'm
a collectible.

With the statute of
limitations all run out,
am I liminal

in the court-light, bare
ly visible on filmy
evidence—a year

the lime of time licked
clean. I did and didn't wash
in the mikveh from

my public body
the baby's bloody exit,
finger prints of post

-office clerks, grocery
checkers that sanctified my
belly-me on both

sides of 16th street
in Washington, DC—the
law's blurry here. Was

holiness washed off
or on in that room (I glow
too hard, blind justice

and I hate to be
fixed on film) but you, the ex
pert of legal thresh-

holds knows *holy* means
reserved for special use, off
-limits to the pub

lic, as in: a
body in a sacred bath.
The secular is

the mirror of the
sacred, the mikveh's ante-
chamber. So maybe

you were just glancing
in the mirror when you saw
me, before the stat

utory dust rag
swiped the image. My belly's
shined like slick steel since.

Thus what you saw was
n't me. The prosecutor's
on the phone (me: "re

habilitation?
she: no, he'll do time). I've year
-missed the chance to ask

what it means to make
somebody already fam
iliar with what time

does and doesn't do,
(the video recorder,
of course, an alarm

ing clock, flicking red
numbers like a dealer) do
time? But as a you

your observer self
was outside time and space be
fore—so it's fit that

one whose eyes entered
forbidden bodies unbid
be bound in a cell.

Which is the smallest part of
a woman's sacred body.

as we settle into our lives like beasts in their ample stalls

Shmuel Ha'Nagid

And I said no to the cleaning lady no I said to carpets
and no to property and property taxes and no to dog
ownership no to Avi's *we'll talk tomorrow* what I meant
was if I had an ample stall I would settle gladly into it
but no I don't I said no to beasts in stalls and I said no to
flowers blooming where they are planted no to tides
and lunar cycles orbits planetary underpinnings retro-
grades and granules of anything and no I said to ero-
sion and shoe polish no to Wordsworth and his non-
fretting nuns and I said no to the spiders and their
sonnet-seeking flies and no and no to the Old Lady
who Lived in a Shoe and no to Prozac Valium Xanax
and the o kept getting larger until it didn't fit into my
mouth no to the second-hand car no to picture frames
glasses frames and pockets no to half-assed apologies
and their paltry cousins white lies and no to Beatrice
and no to midway through anything and no to Laragh
and no to Laragh's proletariat mother who is the actual
Queen of England's actual make up artist and no to
parentheses and no to the never and no to the less no to
making do no no no no no no no no

Family Friendly River Park, San Antonio

Welcome! This is a family friendly river park! For your safety and the safety of the water, please observe the following regulations. This is a family. This is friendly. See the ducklings paddling at the precipice of the dam? Do not use your empty beer bottles as weapons. Honor your father and your mother. Honor the local gods. Grow tomatoes, squash, corn, and potatoes. Do not fornicate more than you can help it. Crush some cochineal. If fornication results in the birth of a child, raise it. In order to have a family of your own, you must be asked certain questions at some point in your life. Or you must ask them. The answer must be yes, eventually. Welcome! Welcome little vulture family with the grumpy adolescent, tail feathers scraggly in the wind. Welcome, calm mama vulture, black and sleek. Soon we will spread our wings. Soon we will comb the wind and learn the currents. Soon something will die. Welcome! As you can see, we are friendly here. We believe in families. We are sorry if you do not have one, but maybe, god willing, one day you will, too. Do not curse in your speech or in your tattoos. Say good morning. Say how are you. Say good afternoon. We are very friendly, very kind.

II. God Box

God Box

One day I bring my daughter from our home in Washington, D.C. to New York to visit her father and his family for Passover. My daughter's aunt Anna introduced the family to the strangers hovering over the communal table at the kosher restaurant on the Upper West Side: "This is Nagy, my mother, and Jacob, my brother; this is my brother's baby daughter, Amalia, and this," she hesitates, then nods toward me, "this is the mother." It feels exactly like a slap. And just as unexpected.

Earlier that day, Anna had cornered me in her kitchen and quietly and efficiently informed me that if I did not marry her brother, she'd not open her "pocketbook, [her] heart, or the hearts of [her] children" to me.

[Of course these are not their real names]

* *

I announced the pregnancy to my family through the postal service with ultrasound images pasted on homemade cards. My parents called, but to inquire, "Are you going to marry?" I said, "Why don't I bring him to meet you, then I will do as you say." My parents said, "I never thought I'd ever tell a child of mine this, but…" and I felt relieved.

My brother and his wife said, "It's good you're having the baby and not getting an abortion. But if you don't marry the father, then you should put the baby up for adoption. It's immoral for you to raise the baby alone, out of wedlock."

* * *

I'd always found that word sinister, *wedlock*. It reminded me of the phrase "kept under lock and key," and I invariably thought of rifles and hard liquor. But when I looked it up, I found that *lac* is an Old English noun-suffix meaning "actions" or "practices" or "proceedings." There were about a dozen compounds formed from the suffix *lac* originally, such as *feohtlac* or warfare. But *wedlac*, meaning "pledge-giving," is the only word that survived with its suffix.

Growing up in rural Texas, I had known about single mothers the same way I knew about snow and maple leaves, skyscrapers and subways—I'd read about them in books.

* * * *

To be swept off one's feet—this metaphor does not come from the motion of a broom. Nor does it come, lamentably, from a long practice of gallant young knights lifting brooms from their girls' hands and saying, "From now on, I'll do the sweeping. My love, go braid yourself some flower wreaths."

I offered Jacob the choice of not claiming paternity, and I promised him he'd never hear from me or my baby again.

Jacob is an immigrant to America. His own father was the only survivor out of seven siblings, and he survived five camps. Another brother died next to him, in the fifth camp, at liberation. We were on a train through Hungary when he told me. I was five months pregnant. I'd accompanied him to see his one uncle remaining there, his mother's brother. His mother and her two brothers survived in orphanages run by Catholic nuns.

* * * * *

My daughter *sweeps me off my feet* in the way things are swept up or away by the wind or by a wave of the sea. Sometimes she knocks the air from my lungs and the floor from under me. Even from the minute she was born I lost autonomy.

It had been a difficult birth. Ten hours of a single constant contraction. I was yelling in pain.

"Quit being dramatic," my mother commanded.

"You—outta here!" I dramatically countered.

She left. Good mother.

"Okay, five more minutes and your baby's dead. Can we operate now?"

These days my daughter and I take turns being the drama queen. She gets Monday, Wednesday, and Friday.

* * * * * *

When visiting my parents I sometimes lie when neighbors say, "Oh, you have a baby! I hadn't even known you were married!"

* * * * * * *

I have felt what I call a blood bond with my grandparents. Not its institutional expression, its conservatism, but its love. And love is a radical element that legislatures and conventions cannot control. The bloodline that holds us together is also the invisible line that the soul navigates, freed from time and space.

One night my grandfather found me in Germany and came to me in a dream, in his blue striped bathrobe and his tan house shoes. "I'm coming to tell you I am dead," he said. I felt him everywhere when I woke up; I still do.

My father phoned from Texas a few hours later. "I know," I said before he uttered a word.

* * * * * * * *

Today, in Tel Aviv, my five-year-old daughter is draw-
ing. Suddenly she circles furiously, in black, all over the
page. She is drawing a picture of a God box.

"A God box," she explains, "is this thing here. And
whatever you put inside of it becomes part of God."

If I were a better person, this would be the last thing I
ever write about my daughter. She has told me not to
write about her again.

My daughter is named for my great grandmother. I am
named for my grandmother. We are all eldest daugh-
ters. In Hebrew my daughter's name means "a work of
God."

Elsa Schiaparelli, Miuccia Prada, Amalia, and Me, at the Met

... with some difficulty [I] obtained seeds from the gardener,
and these [I] planted in [my] throat, ears, mouth...
Elsa Schiaparelli

To have a face covered with flowers would indeed be a wonderful thing: bright, metallic insects around the chosen throat, and sprays of crinkled roses in the hair, to wear a shoe on my head, to cover my shoulders with monkey fur. My daughter is drawing the clear plastic shoes with the plastic pink heels and plastic tears of chandelier pendants (Prada) and the pink dress, with butterflies, she pulls my journal from my hands. *Write* pink *on top,* she commands. All her models accompanied by babies, babies in bellies in dresses, like her father's wife's. Her favorite hat's the lynx head and paws, with its jaw opened, blood on the chin.

To have a face covered with stars would indeed be a wonderful thing, a constellation on your naked chest, to have spilled a cosmos onto your dinner jacket, to have been lifted by buoyant shoulder pads through ambiguity. *Men respect strong women. They do not necessarily love them.* Schiaparelli should know. *I want to stay here forever with Daddy* says my daughter. *I know. I'd love to stay here, too. Not to go back at all again.* I agree.

To have a mouth full of seeds would be a wonderful thing, to be drowned, a throat filled with hard, shiny points, like the mark left by the tip of a pencil, poised on a page. *No, I mean to stay with Daddy. You can go back.* Said Miucci Prada, *the women who wear my clothes vary dramatically. Of course, I'd hope they were clever and interesting. I'd also hope that my clothes made their lives a little easier, that they made them feel happier. Not more beautiful, necessarily, just more of a person.*

Oh, if that's what you want, that's fine with me, I say, splaying the Prada quote across my notebook. Does feeling like a person make life easier, happier? *Really? You'd just let me go away from you?* As a paperweight, I was always being told that I was too fickle. As a place-holder, I was told I dressed too *personally.* There is no correct response. *What do you want me to say?*

That to have a face covered with black netting, a doll hat, a chest, an armor against *amour* and its aftermath, would be a wonderful. To have a face covered with but-terflies, to have butterflies in the stomach, across the shoulders, over the groin, over the kneecaps like scabs. *I want you to say you would not let me go.* They created hard chic and naïve chic and ugly chic. And zipper means *lightning close*—Schiaparelli designs hers from electrical cords. *I wouldn't let you go.* Some of Schiapa-relli's buttons (naïve chic) are acrobats. *Well, I'm going anyway. Goodbye.* I like those best.

Checkers, a parable

When I move here, next to you, you will swallow me up. And when, by stealth, you allow me to draw near, I will swallow you. The object is to move myself past you and inhabit the spaces where you've been. By you I mean, of course, these—I don't mind, I'll take the darker ones. You have whiter teeth. It is genetic, I think. Then we crown ourselves, sitting in the other's past. In this game, there is no tie. One of us will win. The swallowed one is called the defeated. The defeated is weightless, but the victor is standing in the place the defeated left already when the game began.

III. Ordinary Water

The Pigeon, the Washing Machine, the Laundry and the Folk story

"You have to get rid of it," Tali says, gesturing towards the pigeon's nest in the flower boxes on the balcony, "otherwise you'll never be able to hang laundry out there again, not to mention the lice." "But what to do with the..." I trailed off delicately, with a glance at my five-year-old daughter, dressed in a pink princess costume and hovering over a piece of angel-food cake covered in cherries. "I know," says my daughter, looking up from the cake, "you could take the egg and just *throw* it down and *smash* it!"

I have recently acquired a washing machine in Tel Aviv, a city devoid of laundromats. Mine is a German front-loading model, an AEG Lavamat W820. It is about fifteen years old and quite small—I can do one pair of jeans, one poofy princess dress, a large bath towel, a couple of shirts and a couple of pairs of undergarments per load. In its final spin cycle, it shakes so hard that anything you've placed on top will be flung across the bathroom, and the machine itself will have scooted several centimeters across the floor.

We learned not to hang laundry on Friday mornings when the neighbors cleaned their floors. Israeli mopping consists of tossing a bucket of sudsy water on the cement or tile floor and pushing it through the apartment with a rubber mop, then squeezing it through a hole in the corner where it drains outside. The hole is, of course, centered over the laundry lines, and our freshly washed clothing would often be rinsed in dirty, soapy cleaning water. We'd have to wash all over again. If we do not remove the laundry before sunset, it becomes spackled with whatever fruit is in season— ficus fruit, mainly, processed by and squirted from the backsides of the cooing doves with names like rock pigeon, stock dove, laughing dove, Namanqua dove, ornate collared.

And of course, there are the bats—teethy fruit bats, awkward angels.

When I am not doing laundry myself, I am translating folk stories and poems about laundry, mostly from nineteenth century Bohemia and Moravia, and mostly by K. J. Erben.

During one of my research trips, I fell in love with a 90-year-old woman in a remote village in Southwestern Moravia for the combination of long underwear and ruched skirts on her laundry line. It's true that she was cruel to the dog she had tied under the oak tree next to the door; her house had no running water; she had a wood-burning stove. The twentieth century might never have come and gone, which, in that part of the world, may have been a blessing. She had planted rows of onions, potatoes, and spinach up and down her hillsides. Once I came to see her with her daughter and granddaughter, who was my age.. She informed us all that when she died she wanted to have them pour cement over her grave, because surely no one would take the trouble to visit her grave and keep it up when she died, and she didn't want to be humiliated. She also called me a sissy for refusing a third shot of schnapps at 10 am. She was a self-reliant woman who had once been very beautiful. To have survived her beautiful youth without a washing machine must have taken this kind of inner strength, if Czech fairy tales are any indication of the various of dangers that lurk for beautiful girls near outdoor washing sites.

The most popular tale, "The Water Sprite," opens with
the title character sewing himself a wedding costume,
and scheming to marry a particular girl as soon as she
is in his power—near the water.

At dawn the young girl rose,
made a bundle of her clothes.
"At the lake, my mother, sweet,
I'll make my clothing clean and neat."

"Oh no, sweet child, not to the water!
Stay home today, my little daughter!
A strange dream came to me last night.
Oh, stay inside and out of sight."

…
She is so restless, restless daughter,
something draws her to the water,
to the water, nothing she knows,
nothing she longs for. Still, she goes.

As her first cloth touches the lake
the bridge beneath her begins to break.
Down she goes, just like a pearl,
and water closes over the girl.

From below, the waves roll in,
a ring is spreading wide and thin.

The image of that single, wide, thin ring spreading is appalling…I see it slow and silent—the newsreel blank, for it's too awful to write what just happened and too late to do anything about it. And so very easy to have prevented. Now a baby is going to have to die horribly by the end of the tale.

I never liked using public laundromats. I have a resistance to indoor, public places in which electric-powered machines turn round and round. I avoid gyms for the same reason. I suspect I would have loved banging my basket of wet clothing over rocks with the rest of the crones in pretty rivers. I spent more time at the ancient stone washing-house in my French aunt's village than I did in the vineyards and cathedrals combined.

Sapo Hill in Rome is named for soap.

Cleanliness is close to godliness, said the American inventor of the washing machine, James King (whose name sounds suspiciously like King James).

The first washing drum was built in 1857. It was still hand powered.

The first washing machine was a birthday present from one mid-western husband in Indiana, William Blackstone, to his wife in 1874. I wonder if the novelty of it made up for the fact that he was, in fact, giving her a household appliance. I wonder how old she was, how long they'd been married, and what she'd been doing to make him want to keep her away from her girlfriends at the communal laundry rock. Or what he'd been doing.

Washing machines seem to have come into vogue in the 1950s in both Europe and America, along with top 40s charts, which means songs and stories about rivers, laundry, and love disappear after that. I can think of only one such post-washing machine song, *Tonada de la Luna Llena*, by Simón Díaz, the Venezuelan singer/songwriter who left our world in 2014. This ethereal tune, covered later by the Brazilian Caetano Veloso, showcases the violence of necessity, suggesting that the cleanliness of laundry is never more than a cover for the inherent bloodiness and destruction of love. The song opens with the speaker watching a cocoi heron who has been pulled into the river current while hunting for fish, and is now fighting for his life. "This is how one falls in love, your heart with mine," the speaker notes. The short *tonada* ends:

The moon is looking at me
but I don't know what he sees.
I washed my clothes last afternoon,
they are clean (translation mine).

Between the first and last stanza, the speaker has enjoined a boy to run home and get a rifle to kill the chicken hawk that's getting at the hens. If the speaker is a man, the laundry cleanses the clothes of rival blood. But do men do laundry? I'm not sure if it's permitted in fairy tales or folk songs—he probably means he had his clothing washed. And if that's the case, the man's wife must have a washing machine, because I don't think the things would be dry by now otherwise. A former roommate and I would regularly use her salad spinner to press the water out of our dainties, otherwise they'd have taken at least a day to dry. And these dainties were rather filmy and lacy. Much heavier are the clothes of a jealous cattle worker on the Venezuelan plains.

If the speaker is a woman, then perhaps the river exposes the idea that human character is never capacious enough for the violence of human passion.

A washing machine compensates for that—with a machine, we no longer suffer the consequences of our impulses—we do not fall prey to water spirits, for example. And those of us who symbolically do fall prey, for example, unintentionally single mothers like myself, are able to find joy in our child, rather than the madness, poverty, and suffering of the fairy tale mothers who are cut from their communities. Especially in the child who commands us to sacrifice the bird's nest rather than our own.

Reading Nemcova Bozena's *The Grandmother* in Translation

Viktoria, once beautiful and happy in a village that lives in the pages of Bozena Nemcova's book *Babicka*, was strong as a boy, songful, skilled in domestic labor, laughed all day. The boys, of course, were crazy for her. She refused them all.

In Polish stories, also, heroines suffer most who most say no to local boys. What do they want? We are not told. This morning's garden filled with apples burst from heat, tomatoes split. Jim says heat resistant varietals will persist. Seek local.

I cut the last grapes, sweetened in hot shade. Who will eat them now you're gone? The avocado tree you broke is bearing fruit, the wrong banana tree you planted thrusts a scarlet heady bloom, one sees miniature bananas curled like fingers in a sleeping fist.

In Nemcova's book, Viktoria's days end in water. She has drowned, and drowned, singing, her baby. The scoundrel soldier has disappeared. The village called him that, and she, whose animal last days howled lullabies moonrise to moonset on the river banks beyond the village forests rests now.

Nemcova's *Babicka* blesses her, herself, crosses them, marks the spot on page 372 where Viktoria plunges into black-inked waters, between commas, expanding rings, now she is everywhere.

I am setting out this plate of grapes for her lost mouth.

The Brothers Grimm

In the Brothers Grim version of the Water Sprite of the Lake, a man so distraught about his failed business enterprise he's failed to see his wife's nine months pregnant, trades the first born of his house, thinking *kitten, pup,* for restored wealth.

It's not a kitten or pup; it's a *baby.* The baby is taught *stay away from lakes.* He's good with guns. They relax. He becomes a game keeper. Crises overcome.

In the end the boy falls to the lake, of course, just after he has married, of course. And to his young new wife, when she finds him, in the clutches of the pretty green water sprite, he swears he wants to come home.

The wife throws the comb, the flute, and finally the spinning wheel. They are living in an agrarian economy, so I imagine the household is ruined after that, but so is the lake.

I like it that no one suffers quietly. The lake erupts. Man and wife are changed into toad and frog until the waves slowly draw back. Returned to human form, they've been separated. They've lost each other to distance again.

On a dating site this morning I meet an Algerian chef, a Russian ballet dancer, an Israeli kung-fu instructor, a professor of jazz. I am looking, too, for my husband. But I don't own a spinning wheel, and I don't remember what I thought he'd look like. I'm offered lessons of various kinds.

The wife in the story cries, hearing a shepherd play a flute. By now she is a shepherdess, too. "The last time I blew a flute…" she tells him. That's how they recognize each other. The story ends there, in stunned bliss, page 467 in the *Collected Tales*, or, as I call it, the third tequila,

after floods, protests, rallies, bombs, and eclipses, and it's strange that newspapers haven't covered it yet when they've covered everything else that I've done as a collective of a nerve center.

IV. One Bird or Another

Getting a Get

It occurs to me now that there is another genre of fairy tale—the one in which the young, common girl saves her prince or her family. In the Danish "The White Dove," the dove/princess saves a prince who has been sacrificed by his brothers to a witch. When he kisses her, she turns from a dove back into a woman. In Grimm's "The Seven Ravens" a little girl saves her brothers, who have been turned into ravens by their father's inadvertent curse. In Grimm's "Fitcher's Bird," the egg betrays the hapless women who don't quite trust their murderous husband. The heroine of this story disguises herself as a bird.

No one wants to be a bird.

Yes, you can fly, but you are removed from human company.

And you lack speech.

**

The Get is the Jewish document of marital severance. The word is of two letters, *gimmel* and *tet*, which, The Gaon of Vilna once noted, are the only ones of the Hebrew alphabet that cannot make a word together.

Later the rabbi would fold the Get into a fanciful bird-like design and a beautiful blue-eyed young man would translate the proceedings for me, and my husband would deliver it into my ("they must be passive, your hands") hands, and I would place it under my arm and walk to the door and come back.

It was my husband's "gift" to me.

***

In Erben's folksong "Willow," a husband is so incensed with the fact his wife's soul leaves her body every night to live in a willow tree, he finds that tree and chops it down. She dies. In "Lily" the queen-mother is so enraged by her unnatural daughter-in-law, who is a flower by day, and at night, a woman, she tears down the protective home her son has made his wife. The Lily princess dies.

A romantic hero isn't really much of a hero. By that I mean he doesn't act of his own accord. He is, instead, an object upon which the natural forces and the spirit world act. The heroine is often the medium of communal punishment and edification. She is there to show that we are subject to the forces of the world around us. She is often the means by which a community reaffirms its shared values.

****

Now we were called into the scribe's office. We watched the scribe write the Get in beautiful calligraphy and blow it dry with a hair dryer propped on a plastic binder through which he'd thoughtfully bored a hole, so the thing could stand by itself and not damage the page. Even the sign stuck to his door with shiny tape and written in ink was beautifully lettered in blue marker. My companions pointed out, this scribe really loves his job, takes pride in it.

*****

"Open your hands, palms up, and side by side, like this. Press your thumbs to the sides of your hands," the beautiful translator instructed. He didn't belong in that room. They felt very much like birds at that moment, my hands. They felt like the animals that flitted and fluttered away in Taha Muhammad Ali's poem, "Warning," in which the poet begs hunters not to take aim at his happiness, which isn't worth wasting the bullet on.

"They must be passive, your hands." I let them rest, passively, in the air.

It was an act of complete and vulnerable trust. Trust in what? I don't know.

Then the rabbi folded the Get into the shape of bird wings, fold upon fold upon fold upon fold. Of all the unexpected parts of the morning, that was the most surprising. He gave it to my husband, who placed it in on my passive hands, asking me to accept his "gift" of divorce. I took it on my hands, then placed one palm over the other, as if I had trapped a creature that wanted to fly away. I tucked the Get under my right arm, in my armpit, as the blue-eyed translator had instructed. *I don't want to be a bird. I want to be human, in the company of humans. I want this story to make sense.*

******

I did it. I became the winged creature, albeit with my wings folded now. I walked toward the door, then turned and walked back. *If this were a fairytale, someone would be redeemed.*

After I removed the Get from under my arm, I had to give it back to the rabbi to be filed. I can't imagine how they file them. Do they put them in a cage somewhere? Is there an entire zoo of Get birds? It seems unbelievable that they'd unfold them. But maybe they do.

Astrophysics (one bird or another)

The everything I was before, I am.

The field beyond the kitchen door's littered with sticks. The star-dust gritty over the morning floor. Your cupped hand dipping into me.

All the hair and dead cells I've swept and thrown out, ash trays emptied and garbage—does a word ablaze with sparklers leave a scar in the air?

There was moment in that place we were two mirrors cracked open to the same sky, we were two feathers tumbling over each other, missing the same bird.

The fields still fill with sticks, old trunks; the seeds my daughter collects in her pockets she steals. So much fluff goes into the making that it's a tall order to put it all back once it's out, and I am only one word away, one word out of you, one bird or another bird.

Storks

on annual migrations to Africa, crossing the proverbial red-tiled roofs of Europe or magnificent savannahs on their way back, find themselves in a field of sun-warmed cabbage bulbs screwed into root threads. The storks have no syrinxes and are mute. Bill-clattering is an important mode of communication at the nest. Their nests are very often large and may be used for many years. Some nests have been known to grow to over six feet in diameter and ten feet deep. In south Bohemia there is a stork-nest removal service. Although the nests bring luck, they might sometimes bring your roof down.

It's okay, Pan Dvorak reassured me, as we gazed at his roof soon after his marriage to a house owner, the storks come back, even when you clear the nest. Storks
may change mates after migration; sometimes they may even migrate without a mate. And sometimes, when two people love each other very much, having exhausted their catalog of anatomically possible gestures, and are at an impasse, they open their mouths and out comes a word,   perhaps a little wobbly at first, on its first flight between bodies, through the waiting air.

V. Ordinary Light

Ordinary Light

The first synagogue I ever visited was the Mikveh Israel synagogue in Curacao, a Caribbean island off the Venezuelan coast. I'd been hired to research the 500-year history of the Sephardic Jews who ended up in Venezuela.

It was summertime. On the beach nearby the sand was warm and golden, echoing the outer walls of the synagogue. The sand on the floor inside was cool and white, as were the walls. The arched open windows were lidded with a cobalt-blue glass, the color the sky would become by the time service was over. Service times varied each week with the sunset. I, a recovering Catholic, had found this charming. At some point during the service, I suddenly felt I could breathe. I realized that I must have been holding my breath for the previous ten years.

My life until I left our South Texas family rice farm for university had been circumscribed by light. At sunset I fed the poultry and livestock, as I did at sunrise, before school. The August rice harvest began after the sun had burned off the dew and ended at dusk. But since leaving the farm, light had become abstract to me. There was no longer anything in my life I could not do using the light of bulbs or candles; nothing for which I needed the sun. Part of the gift of this synagogue was the miracle of light, of ordinary light.

There is almost no mention of Hanukkah in the Mishna, the oral Torah, redacted between 180 and 220 CE by Rabbi Yehudah HaNasi. He redacted it because the Jews were being persecuted, and time was passing, and they were afraid that the details of the oral tradition of the Second Temple would be forgotten.

During my years in Venezuela and Curacao, I visited houses in which families lit candles to the Catholic saints every Friday night. I had been hired to research, among other things, the first Bishop of Argentina, who had been born into a *converso* family. During the Inquisition, Portuguese *converso* families had not told their children they were Jewish until bar mitzvah age; they had been sent to Jesuit schools.

So much of the story of the Sephardic Jews of Curacao resonates with Hanukkah. Scholar Reuben Margolis suggests that the Mishna redactors left out mention of Hanukkah because they feared reminding the Romans of the recent Bar Kochba revolt. And for fear of antagonizing the monarchy, who instituted a "don't ask don't tell" rule for the first forty years after the Spanish expulsion, the Jews of Portugal had placed sand on the synagogue floors to muffle the sounds of their footsteps. Today the sand is a reminder.

The Protestant Netherlands were one of the few places in Europe which provided Iberian Jews refuge from the Inquisition, and the Sephardim began to move to Amsterdam after 1600, sometimes two hundred years after their forced baptisms.

Their Jewish identity was evident in their two sets of names. They could also be recognized as crypto Jews because they lit candles on Friday nights; their homes lacked statues of the saints; they did not mix meat and dairy.

From Amsterdam, Jews arrived to Curacao by invitation of the Dutch West India Company in 1659.

My last years as a practicing Catholic, the image of the divinized human male body, hung prominently above the altar in churches, used to cause physical unease. I usually had to leave to avoid becoming ill.

I was suspicious of miracles in institutional settings.

I was suspicious of miracles.

Josephus did not call it Hanukkah but rather the "Festival of Lights." This eight-day festival was initiated to celebrate the rededication of the temple by Yehuda HaMakabi after Antiochus IV Epiphanes had profaned it: "they were so very glad at the revival of their customs, when, after a long time of intermission, they unexpectedly had regained the freedom of their worship." Josephus didn't call it a miracle, but rather, "this liberty beyond our hopes."

Tradition says a single consecrated jug of oil miraculously burned for eight days. But I don't bother that much about the oil.

I don't even need there to have been a guerilla victory led by Yehuda HaMakabi. It could have been, as some scholars suggest, a successful petition that led to the re-sanctification of the Temple. It's enough not to have to worship humans as gods. It's enough to have religious freedom. It's enough to have peace and not war. It's enough to have light.

Nissim Gaon suggests the Mishna did not mention Hanukkah because the celebration was so common-place there was no need to explain it. Ordinary light is enough.

Parable of the Island, the Sea and the Sandbar

a note on translation and fairy tale adaptation

During the reign of Claudius, the sea hoisted a sandbar, and an island that was twelve miles long became visible.

> —I would say "the sea formed a sandbar," or "raised." How about "caused a sandbar to be formed"?

> —Is the 12-mile island the sandbar, or did the sandbar cause the island to become visible? In the latter case, I'd say that a sandbar rose from the sea, outlining the island and causing it to be visible.

Während der Regierungszeit des Claudius, hisste das Meer eine Sandbank, und eine Insel, die 12 Meilen lang war sichtbar geworden.

> During the reign of Claudius, the sea, a sandbank, and an island, the 12 miles long has become was visible.

> During the reign of Claudius the sea level dropped along the coastal zone, hoisting a 12 mile long sandbar into view.

> During the reign of Claudius, the sea fashioned/ formed a sandbar Island 12 miles long...

>> The problem for me is that embedding the action of the sentence between two commas leads to distracting pauses.

During the reign of Claudius a sandbar, 12 miles long, with nasty stony teeth, leapt out of the sea and lay on the surface of the water. Sunning itself with the sea lions, the sandbar waited for centuries for a writer to get trapped in its sandy shoals and commas.

The sea, angry at Claudius' attempt to rule the known world, created new land!

> Of course, whoever wrote this is denying the agency of the sandbar. It is very hydro-centric.
>
> Unless the sea is simply an agent of change.
>
> Unless the island is an anti-seamite.

The End of Venezuela

i.

By Roraima my fingertips and toes had already sprouted black buds—their parentage uncertain, for my toes had entered the orifices of the wet river bottoms we'd crossed to become who we were when we stood in this space before the mountain face. But the sky had slipped, too, spilled steel pins—we'd called their nubs stars.

Other women grew themselves into jaguars more readily than I. When we came to the city of fireflies, behind the table mountain, my fingertip blossoms began to show—this made me a hostess—and little wings emerged from my hands and feet. Then my fingertips blossomed again under my knife because I wasn't that generous.

Halfway Up Roraima,

the dart frog, the black one, stretched across the stone under the waterfall, beneath the cascade of green parrots. The water would never stop pounding. The frog grew pockmarked with the spray. Each time he placed his foot and pushed the earth agreed to spin.

From the top of Roraima,

the mother of waters, crystal buds were croaking in their milk.
It would have to last us for a very long while.

Roraima, the Mother of Waters,

the baby was crying. All night long it was crying, and into the morning and intermittently through the afternoon. Everyone took turns opening its mouth—the jaguar, the eagle, and the parakeet—so we could continue listening. When we got to the Orinoco's little mouth opened on the table mountain we discovered it was teething.

ii

The little boat lay on its side in the Coro sand. Inside, orange light—through-the-eyelid-skin orange. Its outside was the only blue the sea never is. The sand was white of course. Yesterday I spread a slippery brown cloth over a card table: I wanted to make more land.

iii

Para Caracas screech the bus drivers, *para ti* screech
the parakeets, a garage at the bottom of this mountain
is why. Once climbing the mountain with my bag of
groceries to my home halfway up I met one who lived
in the village remnant that the mountain wore in those
days like a threadbare cap and followed him like a
thread. I don't remember the village now, only the
thread and the sudden surprise of the parakeet, brak-
ing with a screech, screeching against the sky at the
edge of the mountain, at the end of Venezuela.

VI. Ordinary Earth

Be Brave and Eat

The Medieval meal was a party. No one remembers the menu, the ingredients, or course order. "Rich" and "sumptuous" were what diners recorded of successful ones.

I once saw a vomitorium in a medieval Czech castle that underscored the importance of making room for more. Which explains the frenetic crowding of tooth-like tombstones in graveyards: more underneath the most recent bodies.

The memoirists of the time dug cadavers for study, kept detailed records of the living wheat and cherry preserves and venison pie, apples, pears, eggs, and loaves of bread, the gist of the household currency. (Surely it occurred to at least one that death would never happen to him.) The vests, knives, swords, and glass vessels inherited made of death a certain hand-clasp to another who certainly never imagined his account of them merited my reading from across eight centuries.

Be brave and eat, I tell my spirited eight-year-old, by which I mean me. It won't save you any more than my mother's journal in which she writes the names and the fatal illnesses of those who stop for food and fuel at Prasek's smokehouse and bakery on the rural highway 59 to MD Anderson hospital, promising to pray for their healing or their souls, depending on how far advanced their cancer, will save her, death's self-appointed arbitrator, either.

Still when I remember the years I intentionally starved my body till I no longer bled each month, till I was hardly in this world, and had I died my body would have been a leaf's skeleton, without ever having borne a fruit, I understand why I did so, and it's a waste, and shame that we can't always live as paintings by Giuseppe Arcimboldo, our bodies banquets in which ripe fruit never drops, our mouths the berries, our limbs already roots, our heavens seasonal, our seasons always full.

Potatoes

Other sailor nationals preferred
death to eating the spawn of *demon-witch-whores,*
but the Spanish sailors raided the potato stores
Columbus carried back, thereby avoiding scurvy.
You have to start somewhere, and this will do,
since history was created to explain you.
(Columbus's voyage—to add to the mix—
was underwritten by a Spanish salt tax.)

I'd wanted, in this way, to document
that two hundred varieties once grew in Peru
and the Incan Empire created the method
of freeze drying by stamping their moisture out,
exposing them to sun, these *chuño,* and letting
them freeze and thaw, then stamping them again.
That's how Mrs. Orsak's flabby arms came to plop
eventually, a reconstituted spoon of potato pulp

on the square slot of my cafeteria tray—
at 45 cents a subsidized lunch in Texas, 1979.
The potato flakes retain the shine, when shaken
from their box, of the winter Andean skies,
under whose supervision freeze drying was begun.
Sublime Incan utensils formed from native
clay had eyes, and growing from the eye-threads,
roots, and from the roots the heads of gods.

They may be viewed in Lima's Museo Larco
in subterranean store rooms, loose along
the shelves, among the agile os and tongues
of ceramic corpulent couples, whose
flexibility of flesh and morals
caused many such pots to be smashed by conquerors,
who were "mortified," thus rendering this
collection "all the more important." Tonight the eyes

are cut. My father says to do it. He says
that you must cut and let the edges dry.
That if you plant when the cut edge is
moist, it will rot. I remember how we
used to store them in the sand under a house
raised on cement blocks in Texas. How once my
mother crawled beneath, edged her hand into the storage box,
and agitated a nest of baby rattlesnakes.

I don't remember her turning pale and sick,
I recall getting whipped with a leather belt
after crawling there myself. But then I did
not remember how we acquired seed
potatoes either. There were none available
in Tel Aviv last night, so I bought cooking spuds on Basel
street, wrapped in plastic, in oxidized
cardboard, not Styrofoam, and we cut the eyes,

and the indentions that look like eyes, gently
washing the black earth off, and scratching to see
what lay beneath. And saving some, too, to eat,
the parts clean shaven, no eyes. The dumb and
beautiful skin. Catherine the Great also forbade
the peasantry from growing potatoes, then had
potatoes planted on her land, up to the trees,
posted sentries instructed to accept bribery,

and that's how the potato spread across the
Ukraine. In a failed sonnet I once wrote:
Across the Ukraine, tea-stained, broken teeth
tore the flesh; hands pounded it to dough
and boiled it until it sank and slowly rose.
Frederick the Great threatened with knives the noses
and ears of the Irish to force them to plant.
And thus the ground was fertile for the famine.

Then three times a day for eight months, Antoine
Parmentier, French army pharmacist,
was fed only "hog's fodder" in a Prussian
prison. Later, in the gardens of Versailles
he gave Marie Antoinctte a papery blossom.
The scene makes a pretty prelude to the appetizers,
soups, entrées, and desserts he composed
(200 of them) exclusively from potatoes.

King Louis XIV and Marie invited
nobility to dine. Since peasant
cooperation was the aim of this banquet,
peasants were forbidden by parliament
to cultivate potatoes. Parmentier planted
his behind a wall and instructed
his armed guards to accept every bribe,
and to gift potato blossom nosegays to each bride.

He was right, of course, and so were they;
the blossom is diminutive but pretty,
threaded through the hair, a saucy pink.
You wouldn't think
so, if you bought potatoes today,
on sale, as I did, standard shapes
as stout and straight and graded as a girl
who, half a century later, isn't beautiful,

although she can't believe it (you should know
she once was)—but once potatoes were gnarled
as this narrative, with shapes as uncontrolled
as the deities they embodied in their native world.
I bought mine in a red net with a gold
label depicting fries, pale as an old
day because—much time's elapsed since I began—
classroom Hanukkah festivities demand

I send my child with a peeled semblance
of this once-heretical root, domesticated
for latkes. My calendar's terribly reduced.
Parmentier also published his knowledge
of cornmeal, chestnut flour, grain storage,
mushroom culture, mineral waters,
bread-baking, cheese-making,
wine-making.

(He also improved sea biscuits.)
At Montdidier his bronze
statue surveys the Place
Parmentier from its high socle,
while below, in full marble relief,
seed potatoes are distributed
to a grateful peasant
as a present.

I'm roasting new potatoes in their jackets
this morning with sprigs of rosemary
torn from the neighbor's invasive phalanx
of a shrub, and salt from the local sea.

To *be salted with the salt of the palace*
is *to be in the employ of a king,*
and for five years I've been salted with the salary
of Tel Aviv. Sometimes I forget about the sea

that every evening swallows its pink balled sun
where the mouth of the Yarkon River joins the port,
while, on threads along the Park Hayarkon,
circus performers climb and spin and drop.
The river's mouth is probed by a cone
of light from Tel Kudadi, a Bronze-age fort
guarding this twist in the ancient Via Maris
in which I live, between Memphis and Damascus.

The rosemary, too, means dew of the sea,
from *ros* and *mar,* which explains why it won't
remain within my neighbor's garden boundaries,
though I strike with shears when it begins to choke
my (also native) greens. On every coastal
road the fragrance runs ahead; inland from the valley
of Gehenna to Jerusalem's walls, which Romans once rent
till no two stones stood. Ascent's a scent.

What I like best about the Incas of Peru
was that they calculated time by how long it took
to roast a potato in fire. Who
knows how large the potato, how hot
the fire, if days were long and years were short then, too.
And here I am now, joining time and money through
the roasting of a potato in salt, the dew of earth
that can't contain itself, that's better than it's worth.

Three Sisters

She's the Cordelia of the three Native American sisters—squash, corn and beans. This "bland one" Europeans scorned was known for her powers of fertility at home by any family in the South with fields. How she was called the darling of the gods, how she was there in the first caves, her scattered stems and skins and seeds, like detritus of love, or simply a day. A gown for every season: In winter she wore brown and orange; in summer she wore yellow, green. Last century, stripped bare and sheathed in cream, a Frenchman called her "Spain's revenge" and threw her in the rubbish bin.

Cinderella's Pumpkin

Little did the people guess, those Oaxacan evenings weaving pumpkin mats—above the cave, the fresh sky big with unborn gods—that seven thousand years later this fruit would clutch the coals the devil gave to Stingy Jack, who, failing to achieve heaven or hell, burned through turnips, beets, potatoes, back and forth across the Anglo world. It's just as well they didn't know, since people get the gods they merit. Cinderella waltzing in her starry shoes among the rich hodgepodge of mice and ladies far better filled her own pumpkin than Stingy Jack did. But maybe they knew.

Okra

Long green velvet stars with milk-white pearls for seeds, they
thicken soups and stews with their sheer and sticky silk. Okra
came to us from Africa with news our language has forgotten.
Fried in cornmeal, the pearls recede, a housedress, then, and
beads of sweat, and—why not?—a tall iced tea. Slaves called it
nkruma and sowed the fields their masters owned. They visited
the parent plants in death and flying dreams just off the shores
of temperate seas across the ocean cemetery. Gather, bind us,
gather us, against the produce stores of history, their sold-out
countries.

The History of the Pea

(the Princess and)

A pea-sized shadow cast by his doubt gathered the corners of my world and shook him out, like the crumbs of summer picnics, like the grains an oyster swallowed. There's a knot inside my chest. There's a dent the shape of a pellet at my back, the kind that's scattered through a field of peas to kill the partridge and the crow. Luckily they placed a pea beneath my mattress also, and at dawn the prince will gloat, my purity is proven in my pain. But if I could, I'd be so dull from use he wouldn't even register as a loss. The crown descends upon me like a vise; his fingers curve, my life is circumscribed.

(the secretary of the United States Chamber of Commerce; the Sicilians, and)

There is nothing so innocent and so confiding in its expression, as the small green face of the freshly shelled pea. Asparagus is pushy and bossy, lettuce is blowsy and loud. Radishes are playful and gay, but the little green pea is so helpless and friendly that it makes really sensitive stomachs suffer to see the way he is treated on average at home. Just fling him to water and leave him to boil—and that's that, said William Wallace Irwin, secretary of the United States Chamber of Commerce. Before that, on March 31, 1282, Sicilians rebelling against the French, murdered anyone who couldn't say chickpea—*cece*—in Italian.

Alexander's Plum Groves

The branches of the purple plum sway against the wind more now than ever since Alexander came, saw how far away home was, sprinkled the Mediterranean with plums that cast their silver over all the rounded hills. Then the twiggy groves shed their rosy little suns. Inside the window sills the shadows of luxuriant plums bed them tenderly. Tell me now, how is that wind, what happened to the distance it transverses, the cliffs, the shards of rain, the fist, the knuckles whitening on limbs along the roadside? *Write me.* I'm so hungry that the air will peel itself like fruit as I pass by.

Lantana

Sorry about the haunting; I miss it, though, home. So I'm sniffing heat-split tomatoes, their splashed seeds, their earth, and the great ships of squash I'm loading onto the bike basket, plus there's a daughter who won't weed. Sometimes I think the haunt who laughed at my believed-ins, palming the closet light and leering, was once a man.

The wind breathing into my adolescence, the moon-light, might have been poison the crop dusters dropped; I caught it in my hat, my orange polyurethane flag over my head, my father's matching flag in step with mine across the field, marking the path for Marion flying overhead dropping clear crystals. Hard rain between NASA and the Bay City Nuclear Power Plant where we lived in the puddle pirated by Laffite, the Gulf of Mexico. Cancer coming for everyone. But our haunting wasn't that dread of the day I'll hear the brother with six, for example, children; too, I think my daughter old now enough to remember me in case. Friends say my life, it is blessed, not everything wanted, but who knows what drudgery, war, murder, or casualties of petty jealousies managed to escape me completely unaware and which ones this little act right now implicates or extricates

—I spend several days a week on this because if you let things go, the weeds take over in the garden. Though in Tel Aviv Eitan says, *Relax, we aren't farmers, we're weekend gardeners.* I'm coached on how to control systems I had no idea existed but trust their symptoms. I used to be more lonely and ecstatic, bound as I am these nights to home so that the midnight sea doesn't exist anymore for me, nor the stars so thick they used to press me into bed, rewire my head before I had a girl of my own.

That's lantana, I say walking my girl past their tiny paper plates of various colored flowerlets gathered into a single stem. I know that scent, the smell of sweat and of tomato vines. *No it's not poisoned. We have it at home,* I say, meaning Texas.

VII. Undo the Sky

Theories of Time in the Novel.
A November Tale

In the morning a leaf is missing, the hair of a stray dog flutters on the barbed-wire fence. Night fades to day and day grows dark, your fingerprints slide from my body. Cups collect in the kitchen sink. The year has started to shed its sun; your body does not drop. The hole that fills with dirt

is not for your body. It is for the immigrant who dumped me here. You are on a train to Vienna, riding tracks of ink. You do not even know where you are going, you think you are leaving. You will hear floor-board creaking over there under love on the stairs behind certain doors. That is us. You will hear the floorboards creaking goodbye. It is a night that takes away tomorrow. The morning station fills with smoke, with the tick of diabetic feet, the click of a falling arm. Then the flashing lights of railroad crossings sugaring the blood. I was wrong. The hole, it is for your body.

There is prairie grass surrounding it stitching its edges closed. Sometimes the sky twitches. The air is torn by wire. How many nights till that possession, alone with her joints knotted up she'd wait. She finally told him to go ahead and die. She used to be my grandmother and now she is probably the *I*. One day she will be the *you* because we've been reading too long aloud until the baby grew up and then silently. Must it have taken. Filled her mouth then he left. I used to imagine him

making love on every staircase, behind every door,
every time the 3 am train. Which

one of us do I mean this night that takes away tomor-
row, our cries blowing through your empty clothes as
you enter a certain street—the one with my immi-
grant's dance hall, the one with my family pub. You
don't know how often you will kiss me each time you
open your mouth in the dust that rushes to your
tongue.

Guessing Your Way In

To get here today I have to think about things I don't like thinking about. Namely, my father, an A1, just out of high school, three months married. Me—I was conceived in panic, no doubt.

To get here today, it wasn't necessary that all four boys with whom my father boarded the bus to boot camp two years later be dead, though they were. *It's not my fault*, and *forgive me* I'd mouth to the shiny black mirror of the Vietnam War Memorial on the Mall every Veterans' Day the five years I lived there, but Yusef Komunyakaa has already written that poem.

To get here today I had to believe in the difference between causality and correlation, as I argue in this family court for full possession. For comic relief, I'm talking with Vince about the "Texas's Modern Hispanic Gentleman" ad for Ketel One vodka in this month's *Texas Monthly*: *Get a guy in there with a fedora and a guy with a bow tie and maybe a mustache or a goatee. Yes, a goatee. Well one goatee and one bow tie. Make it red.*

The ad screams demographic marketing on behalf of people who are guessing their way in. *I feel that way all the time*, I concur. *But I'm not as photogenic about it, that's for sure.*

Everyone feels that way. I mean, *what do you wear when you look at Aurora Borealis? I just don't know.* Vince says he swears he heard that conversation.

It's nice to know somewhere someone has that problem. It makes me happy. Like the time my cat got hit by a car and my father had to take her to the fence with a gun to *put her out of her misery*, and I was shocked into a kind of understanding to see my father's face covered in tears.

That explained his anger whenever I cried over butchering the calves. He'd never have survived the war.

Undo the Sky

Leave your guidebooks and home, and measure instead the rate at which the bulbous blue sky bounces itself slowly up and down on the tightrope of the power lines by the highway, the nuclear power plant plunging daggers until the trees close ranks, the rail road scattering its ties like a child, the crop dusters buzzing all over the sky of fields left out in the sun too long. I have looked to the clotheslines to see what long johns, dresses, bikini tops and how far I've come from Texas after all this time.

Now comes the inevitable moment we remember Marion, kindly crop duster who folded a dollar once into my nine-year-old palm for doing such a good job pacing the fields beneath him, holding a red flag, while Ordram fell from the tanks of the plane. How his biplane flew years later into the power lines. His neck sliced like a horizon. His head falling like a sun.

How his name, Marion, after the Mother of God, foretold his plane would one day be pregnant with eternity.

My poetry I believe is located.
It is I who is not

1.

Located. Necessarily. Not necessarily located.

It feels as if the etymological root *Locute* should be related to *Locate*, because what you are allowed to say, what you think to say, depends a great deal on where you are and who you are talking to and who else is listening (i.e. why you are talking).

Like many Texas-born, my mother tongue was not my mother's tongue.

Or, rather, it was by the time I was born, because my mother, having learned English in School, soon forgot all her Czech except for the rosary and a few phrases.

It was patriotic to forget.

All four of my grandparents got to Texas because the Republic of Texas was advertising heavily in Central Europe for white people to come to settle the land, anticipating the *Tejanos* withering, after the Mexicans had been kicked out and the American Indians had been killed or gone. The poverty was wretched in the mountainous regions of Silesia, and in Valassko they had overlords of their own to deal with. They kept the newspaper advertisements for a long time.

It took a long time to get money for passage—my family showed up in the 1900s.

2.

I was haunted by a particular spirit on the rice farm on which I grew up, on the land that my farmer father bought from one of the original 300 Stephen F. Austin Families, white settlers in Texas.

"Did you see the spirit?" I'd ask my brothers and sister and parents.

"Since there are no such thing as ghosts, I know it's just my imagination," they'd answer.

I grew up wondering which murdered nation it had belonged to, and also, how La Malinche, Hernando Cortés's translator, felt after the conquistadores had destroyed her people. But then I'd wonder, which people were hers—since she'd already been betrayed by her mother before she went over, or was sold, to Cortés. What loyalty had she owed? And why do we equate land ownership with innocence?—or at least prior land ownership with goodness? Wasn't her personal lot better with Cortés?

Better to admit it—we don't really value innocence and goodness, but we don't want anyone taking our land, or living on land that we want. And yet, where do women come into the picture?

Because women historically didn't inherit land—they were given, like land, and possessed.

They were vessels, like translators, haunted by ghosts and language.

3. As my body moved over different lands, Venezuela, Germany, Czech Republic, and now Israel, and different languages flowed through my mouth, I became a literary translator and sometimes simultaneous interpreter. I wrote "La Malinche's Love Songs to Hernando Cortés" pondering the almost unmentionable fact that sometimes—often—national interests conflict with feminist ones, meaning personal ones. After all, a woman was historically meant to be a vessel, just like a translator is.

4.

My nine-year-old daughter's native tongue—Hebrew—
is not mine. And also, my Facebook Sulak "friends" tell
me (as did my Czech friends when I lived there) that my
surname is Turkish. It means water—that which flows
across boundaries. And so Czech also wasn't my sur-
name's native tongue—my name was an invader name,
from the Ottoman invasion of Moravia about 300 years
ago. But since they didn't succeed in the invasion, my
surname's presence in Moravia is, in fact, endearing,
rather than annoying. I imagine the first Moravian
possessor of my surname was championed by a trans-
lator, a sort of La Malinche figure, and our line was
born. I wonder about the slippage, though, between the
message the men meant and the one that was received,
transformed, in a new language, by the woman. Some-
times I imagine that translation gave back the original
meaning that had been deformed through conquest.

5.

The thing that is lost in translation is a world, of course, but whose world is it? We often privilege the original statement to an extraordinary degree when the translator is a member of a "conquering" or more powerful culture—maybe in exchange for the land that was taken—but what about when a conqueror is translated? Maybe the translation is the clearer image of the thing the original speaker originally meant to say?

To despair of the meaning of the simplest word—or rather, to begin to live in the idea that words are infinitely expandable and shockingly retractable.

6.

How does one escape this condition?

I'm not sure one can.

Notes

Some of the italicized lines in "Elsa Schiaparelli, Miuccia Prada, Amalia, and Me, at the Met"are taken from the notebooks of Elsa Schiaparelli and Miuccia Prada, as they appeared in the exhibition "Schiaparelli and Prada: Impossible Conversations." The text comes from the exhibition book by the same title, authored by Andrew Bolton and Harold Koda, with an introduction by Jiduth Thurman. MetPublications, 2012.

"The Parable of the Island, the Sea, and the Sandbar" was arranged and curated from comments left on Katja Vehlow's March 20, 2013 Facebook post. The authors of the comments included here are (in order) Katja Vehlow, Dan Joslyn-Siemiatkoski, Joel Hecker, Marcela Sulak, Randy Deshazo, Randy Deshazo, Randy Deshazo, Rachel Harris, Randy Deshazo, Randy Deshazo, Rachel Harris. Used with permission by the post's author.

Acknowledgements

The author is grateful to the editors of the following journals and anthologies for previously publishing essays and poems from this collection, sometimes in slightly different forms with slightly different titles:

2 River: "Undo the Sky" and "Family Friendly River Park, San Antonio"

Asymptote: "The Pigeon and the Washing Machine, Laundry and the Folk Story"

B O D Y: "Cell"

Bouquet [Kytice] K. J. Erben, Translated Marcela Sulak, Twisted Spoon Press, 2012, 2016: "Water Sprite" which is found in the essay "The Pigeon and the Washing Machine, Laundry and the Folk Story"

Colorado Review: "Weights and Measures"

December: "as we settle into our lives like beasts in their ample stalls" and "Reading Bozena Nemcova's *The Grandmother* in Translation"

Diode: "Storks" and "The End of Venezuela"

Gulf Coast Online: "Potatoes"

Iowa Review: "Getting a Get"

Jerusalem Report: "Ordinary Light"

Mudlark: "The History of the Pea" "Alexander's Plum Groves," "Cinderella's Pumpkin," "The Three Sisters," and "Okra"

Oakland Review: "Guessing Your Way In" and "Astrophysics (one bird or another)"

Prairie Schooner: "Elsa Schiaparelli, Miuccia Prada, Amalia, and Me, at the Met" and "Dear Honey Suckled, Dear Fire Department"

Queen Mob's Teahouse: "Drawn That Way"
Rattle: "God Box"
Superstition Review: "Theories of Time in the Novel. A November Tale"
Women: poetry : migration [an anthology] edited by Jane Joritz-Nakagawa. New York: Theenk Books, 2016: "My poetry I believe is located. It is I who is not"

This book would not be possible without the support of the Virginia Center for the Creative Arts. Special thanks to Erika Meitner, Sarah Wetzel, Michele Battiste, Alicia Jo Rabins, Amy Lemon, Kathrine Varnes, Jane Medved, Maya Klein, and Adriana X. Jacobs for their insightful readings of the manuscript and of individual pieces. Thanks to Avi Vardi for everything. Finally, thank you to my wonderful publisher, Diane Goettel.

Photo: Daniel Fainberg

Marcela Malek Sulak is the author of two previous Black Lawrence Press poetry titles, *Decency* (2015) and *Immigrant* (2010). She's co-edited with Jacqueline Kolosov the 2015 Rose Metal Press title *Family Resemblance. An Anthology and Exploration of 8 Hybrid Literary Genres.* Sulak, who translates from the Hebrew, Czech, and French, is a 2019 NEA Translation Fellow, and her fourth book-length translation of poetry: *Twenty Girls to Envy Me: Selected Poems of Orit Gidali*, was nominated for the 2017 PEN Award for Poetry in Translaiton (University of Texas Press). She's also translated Karel Hynek Macha's *May* and Karel Jaromir Erben's *Bouquet of Czech Folktales* (Twisted Spoon Press), and Mutombo Nkulu-N'Sengha's *Bela-Wenda* (Host Publications), from the French. Her essays have appeared in *The Boston Review, The Iowa Review, The Los Angeles Review of Books, Asymptote*, and *Rattle,* among others. She coordinates the poetry track of the Shaindy Rudoff Graduate Program in Creative Writing at Bar-Ilan University, where she is associate professor in American Literature. Look out for her next poetry collection, *City of Sky Papers*, from Black Lawrence Press in 2021.